CHAPTER ONE:
The 13th Warrior
Act one Scene One:Broken Wing

The Ghost Camera Shows Everything,Behind the Scenes,mistakes,and Parts that will Later be edited,gone thru, shortened to make into a Movie.The Old man Talks: "Once Upon a Tyme,a long time ago the Son of Man was Told to find 12 Warriors to Battle the Evil forces that were taking over this World. He was Given 33 Years to Teach Mankind these Truths.The Laws were written in Stone But Our Societies and our Different Cultures would Not Accept these truths and follow them.Why Was The Son Of man Nailed to a Cross In the First Place? What sin Did He do that was so bad they wanted to Crucify Him? They Had to Kill Him to Silence Him,Yes they had a Scam going,Still do. They were making a lot of money off of Gullible People. Everyone knows the Holy Bible is a Bunch of Individual People telling you Their Version Of What they Think Actually Did happen,That is Why Its called a Version. Who's Version Is Correct? Who's Version Is Wrong? Who Gets to Decide? Now over 2,000 Years later society and All Our Different Cultures Still will Not Accept the Truths,Yes over 90% of all the People who Think they are Good Christians Have been Misled,The Blind leading the Blind. What has to Happen to Show the Way?" Pause for Break Early Morning bedroom Scene,The Alarm goes off,He climb out of bed and heads to the Bathroom. As He reach's around the wall to Turn the Bathroom Light on,He rubs His Chin,thinking I need to Shave.He looks in the Mirror as the Camera Zooms in,the Black smoke shows the Demon Entering His body as His eyes turn a Glossy Black. He rolls His head around and smiles. He reachs in the Drawer for Scissors and start cutting all His gray hair off,Then He reachs for the shave cream and gob a lot all over His head.He Shaves everything off but His Moustache.Then He takes His Pajamas off as He opens the Shower curtain,naked He climbs in the shower, closes the curtain,turn the shower on.The Camera goes to a Boxing Arena, a Crowd of People watching a Boxing Match. The Pretty girl in a Bikini walks around instead of Showing round two or Round five she has a Big card showing five minutes later.Everyone is amused. The Shower stops,the curtain opens He steps out and grabs a Towel to Dry Off.The camera zooms in and shows all the New Tattoos on His chest and upper arms. His Eyes are still Glossy black showing the Demon is still Inside of Him. He drops the towel and raises His hands in the air,declaring to all the World the Power He now has. Two large black Raven wings over 4 ft tall appear on His back as they start flapping He rises from the ground. the camera shows His feet are off the ground. Out of no were a lightning bolt appears with a loud thunder, His right wing snaps off,"with a Broken wing" a song by Martina Mcbride is sung in the back ground. He falls to the ground,naked He rolls into a Ball on the floor,He cries out loud,"Forgive me God,Forgive me Goddess,Forgive me Father,forgive me Mother." Thru My Pride and Arrogance, my Wing was Broken. He laid on the Floor,Naked sobbing. the camera Zooms in on His naked back showing the

Broken wing with blood flowing down His back,the other wing folds up as He sobs uncontrollably.A few Minutes go by then the two black wings disappear,the Blood disappears. He grabs the towel from the floor as He wipes His face He reach's with His left hand the top of the Bathroom sink to Pull His self up. His hand shapeshifts into a Demonic hand with long fingernails showing the Entity is still Inside of Him. Then He reach's with His other hand to pull Him self up and it too shapeshifts into a demonic hand with long fingernails only for a moment so the viewer can see the Entity is still inside of Him. as He pulls Him self up,He dries Him self off with a Towel and Then He notices the Tattoos all over His chest and Upper arms. He grabs a Wash cloth and scrub His chest and arms trying to remove the tattoos,He cries out to no one "Is this the Mark of the Beast?" Forgive me Father, forgive me Mother, He sobs to no avail. Finally He puts His underwear and clothes on. He looks in the mirror and the Glossy black eyes disappear only His normal eyes. He grabs the Hair brush to comb His hair and Then He realize's He cut all His Hair off. He brushs His moustache and eyebrows,The only hair He has left. As He put His Watch on He notices the time,"The Camera Crew will Be here soon". He starts to Reach up to turn the Bathroom light off,He pause's in Mid air. Twirl His Fingers around and the Lights go off. He Knows He Now Has the Power." How do I use It? How do I Control it?" He remembers when He was a Alcoholic,the eight words that Helped Him get over that addiction. "You Control it or,It Will Control You." So Now with this New Power Knowing the Spirit World is watching You Have to follow the Eight words of Mother Earth and they are "And You Harm None,Do What you Will," He ponders the Idea that both of the Important Powers now in His Life have Eight Words. Why Eight? He thinks to Him self, Remembering as His Hand Shapeshifted in this Demonic hand with Long Fingernails as He grabbed the edge of the Bathroom sink, are the Fingerprints left, mine or some other Demonic entity? He worked for the Hunt County Sheriff department for ten Years,Mostly He was a Outside Detention Officer which Means He dealt with Only the Trustees, Those who were in jail only 90 days or less. His Job was to use Inmate labor to save the County Money,Mowing, weed eating, Cleaning, mopping etc,minor custodial and Maintenance work. He has watched enough Movies and real Life to Under stand that if this was a Crime scene then they would dust for fingerprints and Any found would be put in the Data base , Everyone Knows this.He grabs His Coffee cup and takes a drink as the Doorbell Rings He walks to the Door to let the Camera Crew in. We Shake Hands and after Introductions She Sets Up her Tripod.One Camera Girl and Her Assistant another Girl both Young and Beautiful climbing the Corporate ladder.They are Unaware of the Ghost Camera for You see No One Can see the Ghost Camera,Is it a Ghost? The Presence running the Lone Camera feels to be another Female,Yes Young You see a Glimpse of Her every once in a While. Now He Has the Power He can Now see Her More Clearly. the Other Two girls are Unaware of the Ghost Camera Filming all the Behind the Scenes activity.We Set Up In The Living room He grabs a Fresh Cup of Coffee and ask the Girls would they like some,"Yes" they replied "do You Have any Creamer like French Vanilla or hazelnut?" Yes He replied I have Both,They Giggled as they made up their Coffee, we stopped for a

Moment to enjoy the Early Coffee Break He remembers when He was Younger Learning a New Trade He chose Electrical Work Because His Older brother and His Wife's brother both were Electricians. He always wanted to get into the Movie Business and that was what these two Young Girls chose. You Have to Start out doing Minor Task learning the Ropes,same with any trade or business.you can not just go up there and tell them you want your High School diploma or Bachelor Degree You have to take the Time and earn it. Just Like in the Army you Can't just go up there and say you want to be a General,again you have to Earn it.He wonders about this New Power He has, Will This Demon appear again? Will His Hands or other parts of His Body Shape shift into this Demonic creature? What about The Raven Wings one was Broken,Yes He felt the Pain courseing thru His Body as if You broke a Leg,the Excruciating pain He did Feel, was it my Imagination? He felt the Blood Pouring down His back as He curled up on the Floor,was all this His Imagination? Yes the Pride, the vanity,the Arrogance He felt the Power as the Wings did lift Him off the Floor. He felt alive and Younger,much stronger but only for a moment. He now Understood the Power of the Angels and Demons if Only for a moment He still tasted the Power and felt it go thru out all of His Body He was alive only for a moment and Now All He has is the memory but How did You turn off the bathroom light by Just waving Your hand? I will Practice after everyone leaves and see if I still have this Power Time will Tell What will I Do with this Gift? Is it a Gift from God or the Goddess or some Demonic force? If I can Shapeshift into this demonic Entity can I shapeshift into something Else? So far only my hands seem to change will other parts of my body change also? I felt this Power surge thru me sort of like when the Wings grew on my Back I felt the power I could actually fly, if only for a Moment, I felt what the Angels and Demons must have felt.Yes, the power was Sensational, the Energy was great, He felt the Power, if Only for a Moment and He will have that to remind Him at what cost? He will Not Forget the Other Power,when Lightning broke His wing off, everyone heard it snap and He felt the Pain. I do Not want to go thru that again Never Again End of chapter One

Chapter Two:
Fingerprints of God/Goddess
Act Two Scene two

She Clips a Microphone to my Shirt and they say "anytime you are ready",the Film starts up as He sets on the couch. "Hello,My Name is Melvin Abercrombie,Author of Twelve Books,some are at Amazon Book Stores,Barnes and Noble and Trafford Publishing.I Titled this Book The 13th Warrior, We Should Start from the start or In the Beginning there Has to be a Big Bang so to me there Has to be Two of something to create this Bang,Right? so for Creation to work there Has to be a Male and a Female to Create anything right? So If we call these two Entities a Male God and a Female Goddess does That make sense? The God/Goddess,In Hebrew He Is Called Yahweh and She is Called the Shekhinah. Of Course Most Religions Today Only Worship a Male God,Then

You Have Your So Called Pagan Religions that do Worship the female side. Does God Have a Fingerprint? Does the Female side of God,the Shekhinah, Have a Fingerprint? Do Angels Have a Fingerprint? Does Lucifer Have a Fingerprint? Do Demons have a Finger print? We Do Know that Jesus Christ Did Live on this Earth for 33 Years,His Job was to recruit 12 Disciples to Help Him Teach Society the Laws and To Fight the Evil,that is Lucifer,The Lord of this World,the Real First born Son and the Ruler of this World. This Is were People get Mixed Up at,You See God the father let Lucifer Rule this World after he was Cast out of Heaven,After a While God Did Look down and saw all the Evil Lucifer was making and Wished He Had never created this World,Everyone Knows this and That is Why The World was Destroyed By Water,Right?So Now Thousands of years later Lucifer was Still Corrupting this World so God,The Father sent down Jesus Christ to Teach Us the Truth so we Do Know He had a Fingerprint,Right?" They Both Shake their heads in agreement. "Everyone Knows about this Male Creator God,the Last Two Thousand Years we, as a Society,as a Civilization, as a Culture Decided to Accept this Male Creator God as Doing all This By His self. What happened to the Female? If We read History Books and Look at all the Other Books out there then we can see the Female side of God still There. Right Now the Fastest growing Religion is called Wicca were You get the Eight words "And You Harm None,Do What You Will." I went thru the 3 Initiations of Wicca thru the Years I ran away from this Male God,with Help from Lucifer and His Demons I was persuaded to Join the Wild side of Life. Most of My Books I talked about this. Has Anybody ever Noticed the Female Statue of a Fertility Goddess on top of Our White House Capitol?" The Camera Girls look at each other shaking their heads." Has Anybody ever Notice the Symbol of the United States is a Female Statue of Liberty?" Again they Both Shake their Heads showing they Never even Thought about this in that way. We go On "What were our ForeFathers Thinking? Could they have Realized That Everything in Creation Did Come from a Female? We Can Look thru out History,the Egyptians,for Example worshipped a Female Goddess known as Isis,She is in No Way associated with this Terrorist Islam Group who Stole Her name. Most Islam along with other Religions of today including Jewish and Christianity do Not Worship a Female Goddess as Equal. If You Really look at most Major Religions of Today then you will see They Have a Male Dominant Creator. Then If you Look at Wicca then you Have a Female Dominant Creator. Were is the Equality? Were is the Balance? Were is the Harmony? We Do Know a Long time ago Most all the Major Civilizations did Have this Equality .Egyptians, Romans, Greek, Teutonic,Celtic and Even native American Indians to name a Few so what happened?" We pause for a Moment showing My Coffee cup is empty,We stop for a Moment,Refill our coffee cups,they Brought some donuts so we take a Short Break,Their Camera is off but the Lone Camera Is still Rolling Showing all the Behind the Scene activity. The Camera goes to The Boxing arena again showing the Same Beautiful girl in the Bikini and showing the same Big Sign saying Ten Minutes Later This Time.Everyone is amused. Back to work He sets down in His Oak Rocking Chair this time,He loves this old antique chair with the 3 Carved Heads on the Back and the Claws on the Hand rails. The

Lone Camera Noticed the Heads moving around and the Claws moving around but the two camera girls and their camera does not Notice this at all. Is it Our Imagination? Special effects? Illusion? what is Reality? The Girls are ready they Motion Him to Start when Ever You Are ready,He Takes a drink of Coffee and sets it on the Coffee Table as He looks in the Camera He resumes His Dialogue. "Where were we? Yes,I remember we were talking about the Female side of Our Male Dominant God. Christian People Today call this the Holy Spirit,The Holy Ghost or the Comforter. If you Go to Your Computer and Google the Words Holy Spirit you will see it is Feminine,same as Holy ghost and Comforter. Why Would Our Computer show this as Feminine?" He pauses, they Both Shake their Heads as He takes another drink of Coffee then set it down and Continue."Did God Create Jesus Christ By His Self?" He Pauses for that to Sink in,the two Camera Girls look at each other Like They Never thought of it in that way Expression. He continues "No,He Had to Go Find a Female Virgin, Right?" He pauses,They Shake Their heads in Agreement so He continues "Did God Marry this Virgin Mary? No,She was Already Promised to Joseph. What Do You Call a Child Born out of Wedlock? This is What Most Islam,Jewish and other Religions think of Our Version of What happened. No Wonder they call us Christians Infidels,No Wonder we are having so many Different Wars and Continuous Fighting. All You Know is What You were Taught.Your Subconscious will Only Accept what you tell it to believe in. They Can Only Teach you what they were Taught. I was Taught from the day I was Born that we are Baptist Christians. My Parents, Grand parents and all My Family were Baptist. This is all I Know,a long time ago they believed Baptist were the Pure Religion Because Jesus Cousin,John the Baptist actually Baptized Jesus with a Full Submersion to Wash away the Sins so the Catholic and others who Teach you can just Sprinkle a Little Holy Water would be wrong and they all would Burn in Hell Forever and ever.You Look around at all the Different Denominations,different Tenets of Faith,different doctrines but most all Worshipping the same Male Dominant God and the Same Male Son of God and calling the Holy Spirit as another Male But all three being one,then Who is on the Right hand side of God? Who Is Intercedding on our Behalf if they all three are one? The Big Question is What if the real Jesus Christ was alive today in Flesh and Blood and we asked Him to go to Your Typical Sunday Church say your Local First Baptist Church, would He go there on Sunday,the 1st day of the week? No Would he Go to Your Local Catholic Church on Sunday? No The Real Jesus Christ Never Worshipped on Sunday the First day of the week,You Can Not Show me anywere in any Holy Bible were the real Jesus Christ Worshipped on Sunday the First day of the week during the 33 Years he was alive. Everyone knows He was Born a Jewish Person,He spoke the Hebrew language. Why Would they call Him a Rabbi? If you went to a Typical Synagogue and Asked to Read the Torah would the Rabbi Let You? No way,Only Those Authorized with the Right Schooling and Certification would be able to go into the Holy of Holies and read the Torah. Say for example you have two People in the army both are wearing the same Green Uniform,one is a Private and the Other is a General,How do you tell the difference between the two? They are both wearing the same shirt,Same Pants,Same boots and same

Hats? One is a Private and the Other is a General how do you tell the Difference? We all Know they have these little Medals on the Private has a one bar Chevron and the General has a Chrome star, this is how you Know Which Person to Salute and Show respect to. When Jesus was walking, the Normal Clothing they wore during this Time frame were Long White or colored Robes so To Identify Him as a Rabbi then He would have a Breast Plate, or Medallion showing He was a Rabbi Just like a Police Officer would be wearing a badge of Authority. This could be Part of What Jesus Christ did do during His Lost Years. Several People on several Occasions did call Him Rabbi Why Would they call Him that Unless they Knew He had the Creditials? He had the Medallion the Breast plate or the Identification so He could Walk into the Synagogue Take the Torah and read from it and the Bible says everyone was amazed" We Stop and take another Break this time for Lunch Their camera Stops But the Lone Camera Keeps Going she Does Not Need to Take a break, She does not eat or drink or go to the Bathroom like we do. She is a Spirit/Soul that thrives off of Energy. Just like a Vampire drinks Blood to Survive She is one of the original VamPowers who Thrive off your Power or Energy, Yes she can go into Human form into another physical mortal flesh and blood human to temporary Experience, feed, drink, and absorb your energy, sometimes thru the sexual act during intercourse draining the orgasm from Her Victims, the Life line of all creation. they lay their smiling, drained and all energy gone not realizing were all the Energy went to. They have to go to sleep to Re-charge themselves then go thru the process over and over not knowing what is going on. The Blind Sheep, who is the Predator? Who Is the Victim? End of Chapter

Chapter Three:
Sons and Daughters
Act Three   Scene Three:

The Old Man Talks:" If you Read the Bible then you Know in Ephesians Paul Talks about Putting on the Armor Of God, Yes Paul Knew there was a Battle between Good and Evil. Most of What Paul wrote about was around 60-70Ad which was a Long time after Jesus Christ was Crucified. What Happened during these lost 30 Years? Most Hebrew Christians were afraid of also Being Nailed to a Cross so they were Scattered. The original 12 minus Judus iscariot went off to different lands to spread the Truths, Did Jesus Christ Ever Worship on Sunday, the 1st day of the week? We will talk about that later on in a different chapter but I want the reader to Know who and what was the Original Yahshua all about, You See The letter J was never in the Hebrew alaphabet still Is Not so the original Name for the Son of man you call Jesus was Yahshua This Chapter is all about the Sons and Daughters of the original God Yahweh and the Original Goddess Shekhinah, This Book Will Prove that the Real Yahshua Fulfills that in every way." Pause He Is Drinking a Glass of Iced Tea, Back in the Living room." Was God a Alien? Did God Come from another planet?" He pauses for that to Sink in and take another drink of Tea."When we Think of Aliens we Think of Little

Green Men with Big Eyes" They Both Giggle and shake their Heads in agreement. He smiles and Continue "so If this Place we call Heaven, were is it? We want to Think of Heaven as some Place up above and this Hell we were taught is Someplace below. Again,All We Know is What we were Taught. If their was a Male God and we Called Him By His Hebrew Name of Yahweh and He Had a Wife,The Holy Spirit,we Call the Shekhinah then they Both thru Perfect Love,Perfect Trust got together and Had Children. We Know they Must of had Children,Who Created Angels? If God Created everything then It would make sense that this Male God did Plant His Seed and Helped Create these Angels Right?" He Pauses for that to sink in and take another drink of Ice Tea "From the Previous Chapter of this Series we Understand that Common sense Proves there Has to be a Female in this Creation Process,Call Her the Queen of Heaven,The Shekhinah, The Holy Spirit,The Holy Ghost.The Comforter ,Isis,Juno,Hera,or what ever Name You Feel Comfotable with Everything in Creation,Every Human, Animal,Bird,and Fish Did Come from a Female. Everything in Creation will Eventually Die and will Return to a Female,We Simply Call Her Mother Earth, Actually I call Her Auriel,the First born Daughter. Remember in Wicca they talk about some other Arch Angels Raphael Rules the east and He is the Air,Michael Rules the South and He Rules the Fire,Gabrael Rules the West and She Rules the Water and Auriel Rules the North and She is Called Mother earth.Now Everyone Knows the Holy Bible Story about a Third of the Arch angels were cast out of Heaven. Were did these Fallen Angels go to? Were are they Now? Could Lucifer be the First born Son and Auriel be the First born Daughter Because of His Rebellion,He was Cast out of Heaven so when you Think of the devil What do you think of first?" He pauses for that to sink in and take another drink of Ice Tea ' We think of Fire so We were Taught that this Hell is somewere down Below, Actually Hell is the Sun(Son) If You Try to land a Rocket ship on the Sun what would happen? Everyone knows it would burn up. Could the Sun(Son) be this Place that Lucifer,the Devil was Cast to? Then You Say The Sun has a Lot of Good also,Yes I agree,the Sun can Burn you,Give you Cancer,Blind you but we Need the Sun to Survive so is there good in Lucifer? Just Like we are created with this good and Evil inside of Us could Lucifer have both Good and Evil Inside of Him? One of My Books We use the Fictional Imaginations of What If after Thousands of Years Lucifer was Tired of playing the bad Guy. So In My Wild Imagination We would Imagine If I was lucifer and was Tired of playing the Bad guy and I wanted to Come back Home,Would God,The Father, Let me Come back? Could I be This Prodigal Son? What If We wanted to Settle Down,Get Married, Raise a Family and even Promise to Go to Church? So We Imagined Who I would Go Into? Of Course the Most Richest,Good looking single Bachelor who Happened to be a Movie star and the Imaginary Grandson of the Famous actor who Imaginary Had a Sexual affair with another Beautiful Actress and a Child was born so anyway its all Fiction just a Wild crazy Idea.So We do Know there is this Guy we call Satan or the Devil or Lucifer what ever Name you want to Call Him and we Know that If He was the First Born son then He would Have the Right to Rebell after Thousands of Years He would Be the Only Person having the Right to One Day Take over This Throne of Power,But Once you realize the Father Never dies so Now What do you Do? You Create this World to Give these Fallen Angels something to Rule over. We Know God,The Father stood back and Let Lucifer rule for a While then the Bible Says that God Looked down and saw all The Evil that was created and wished He would Have never created all This so He Tried to Destroy all This Evil Thru a Flood. Everyone Knows this, at One Point In your Life you probably did go to some kind of Religious school or hear from someone else about this Creation process. Most christians today went to Sunday school because your parents told you that now its ok to worship a Male Dominant Creator God on Sunday,the 1st day of the week.All You Know is what you were Taught,Your Subconscious will Only Accept what you tell it to Believe in..All They Can Teach You Is what they were taught and Their Subconscious will Only accept what they tell it to believe in.Who Is right? Who Is wrong? Who Gets to Decide? When you have Millions, Billions, Trillions of Different people all being taught a Different Language,Different Fingerprint, a Different Religion, a Different Culture, Now You Understand Why There are so many Different Religions when In the Beginning there was Only One Adam and One Eve,What was their Religion? Were they Taught Islam? Jewish? Hindu? Buddah? Christian? the hundred different branchs of Christianity? When You Get to heaven will All These different Religions Be Up there? will There be Jewish Over Here? Hindu Over There? Buddah Way over there and all the Different Christian Religions were wil they all be at? Am I the Only Person Thinking about all this? Remember you have Million,Billion,Trillion different People alive today all with a Different Religion all with a Different Language and a Different Culture again Who is right? Who Is Wrong? Who Gets to Decide? We did Ask the Question that if Jesus Christ was alive today what Church would He go to? Most of the Christian Churchs,today think that now its ok to worship a Male Dominant Creator on Sunday,the First day of the week even Though we Know the real Jesus Christ never worshipped on Sunday,The 1st Day of the week,He did Keep the 7th day Saturday sabbath so you say there are some churchs that do Keep the 7th day Sabbath,Yes and some actually Keep the Kosher food laws but there are None that also teach about the Goddess as a Equal along side of God or Teach Re-Incarnation and most will tell you Do Not worry you are saved by Grace and you will get to go to Heaven when you die so right now its a Shame but there is No Church that Jesus Would go to, so We created the Broken Wing Ministry trying to show People the truth about the Male God Yahweh,The Female Goddess Shekhinah,the Real Jesus Christ,The true 7th day Sabbath,The Kosher food laws and Re-incarnation, You do Not Just die and get to go to Heaven forever and ever. What would the World be like if we had a Broken Wing Ministry Church in every Town,Every City all Over the World? Sure you would still Have your Jewish, Islam,Hindu,Buddah and other Christian Churchs but Is the World ready for one more Different Church? Is the World ready for the True Church? You Decide It takes People Like you willing to read this and say Ok It makes sense I will Help Build a Broken Wing Ministry In My Area or do Not do Nothing ignore this book and we will see what Happens Next." End of Chapter

Chapter Four:
Re-Incarnation
Act Four Scene Four

The Old man is Talking:" I remember when I was a Kid I found this Grasshopper and I put it in a Old mayonaise Jar,I punched holes in the lid and Put some grass for it to eat then watched it.Several Times the grasshopper Tried to Jump up but Hit His Head and finally Quit trying..When I went to bed I could hear the grasshopper jumping up,Hitting his head finally He Gave up.The next morning I felt sorry for the grasshopper so i went outside,took the lid off then said jump out you are now free,a Few Hours went by and I went into lunch after i came back I seen the grasshopper still Inside. he Got Tired of Trying and Just gave up. What is the Difference between a Rich person and a Poor Person? The Rich Person Never gives up,He Keeps on Trying over and over,Even If He looses Everything they Have the Knowledge that sooner or Later they will Finally Achieve what they want. Which One are you? So You Are asking what does this story Have to do with Re-incarnation or what some call Resurrection? You Can Not Possibly do all the Things you want to Do in One Lifetime,Some times you Need to Experience being a poor Person in another Life you Need to Experience being a Rich Person,One Life you need to Experience Being Black,Another life you Need to Experience Being White or Oriental" New Day They Arrive and set Up, this time we are out side.We have a Swimming pool with a Man made waterfall pumping water out of the Pool and Circulating back in and adding the Chlorine as needed. This is Our little Picture of the garden Of Eden,Its a Nice day so we decided to film outside. Everything is set Up.Microphone on my shirt collar ready to go:"This will Be Chapter Four,We already Talked about our Male God and What We believe as the Female Goddess,We agreed they did have Children,someone had to create Demons and Angels So if God Created everything then It would stand for a reason that our Male God Did Create Angels and we Do Know a Third of these Arch-Angels were cast out of Heaven so these became our original Demons or what some like to call Daemons.One of the Big Questions we already asked was Does God have a Fingerprint? We were Created in the Image of God so it would make sense that if He wanted to identify us by Giving us a Unique Different Fingerprint then He would Have one Also. Does the Goddess have a Fingerprint? Does the Sons and Daughters,we call Angels and Demons Have a Fingerprint? so Now If,When we Die from our Mortal,Flesh and Blood Human Body and we are Judged,Do we Carry this same fingerprint with us from one Re-incarnation to another? We Know we have Lived many Past Lives, I have gone into Self Hypnosis and Recall some of my Previous Lives. I was never a King or President or If I was I do Not remember,One Past life I Have had several dreams about so they felt real Did I leave my Fingerprint in My Dream?We know back in the time the Black plague was going on and a Lot of Good People did Die,all My Family,my Wife and Children all did die from the Black Plague,Why was I spared? I Believed I was spared Because during that time I studied The Magical arts some were good magic and others were what was called dark magic I was a Real Vampire which means I did not drink blood but absorb the Energy the Power from my Victims,You would Now call Us Physic Vampires,for you see a Real Vampire Never drinks Blood,He or She is Not afraid of the Cross or the Sun that is all Superstition to fool the common People. We can Touch you and Pull your Energy from You. We can use Our 5 senses and Merely Look at you and My Eyes will Touch you and I can draw your Power from you. If I Hear your voice say even on a Telephone all the way acrooss to Europe i can Touch you thru my Hearing. After all My Family died from the Black Plague I found solace in the Bottle of Rum to satisfy the Demons inside of me only to wake up the Next day, hungry and wanting to feed from a new victim and back to the Bottle of rum to quiet the Demons if only for a While. The People who ran the Ships were Having a hard time getting sailors to Run their ships and the Pirate trade were no different, one Night a Stranger bought me several rounds of Rum and as I passed out, they Loaded me on their Ship,the Next morning I woke with a Hangover for away from land. I had a Choice, Jump over board and feed the sharks or work the Boat. Not Much of a Choice but I wanted to live. They got into a fight with another ship and a Man come running at me with a sword,I had to defend my self or die,I killed him,stole what he had on him including His Nice Sword and tossed his Body over board to the Sharks he would have done the same for me,Killing got easier,at the Time I knew Killing was wrong I grew up as a Christian back then and I knew sooner or later I will Have to make my Peace with my God.. The Ship eventually was hit and we all started sinking every man for him self the captain and a Few of His right hand man grabbed the only few lifeboats i found a Door that was tore off because of the cannon explosion and grabbed it Hoping it would float,It did. I fell asleep on the board and woke up the next morning to a Bright sunny day,no one in Sight,If anyone did Survive they were long gone. I drifted for three days and Three Nights delirous laughing that iam Surrounded by all this food and i am starvin,surrounded by all this water and I was Dying of thirst. I tried drinking the salt water it only made me sick,finally out of desperation I called on this God and Goddess to forgive me. I know I had no right to ask but I accepted My Fate and to weak to stay on I rolled off the board. A Beautiful Naked Blonde woman with blue eyes swam Up behind Me and rescued Me, Even in my Weakness I was Aroused, she was Beautiful,I felt this Must be Heaven,I did Not Deserve this But I am Not Complaining, Finally My feet touched sandy Bottom and I walked a Shore I turned to Get the Woman who Helped me, she waved and swam off,She was a Mermaid, half woman Half fish. I will Never forget the dreams over and over. It seemed so real. I made a Vow to change my ways and I became a Preacher trying to Teach others the Amazing Power of Our Creator God and Goddess. Another past life I was a Outlaw,I was a Very Bad person who Killed and stole from People this was During the 1800's. I fell in Love with this Beautiful red head Who Happened to be married to the Town Sheriff. One Night in a Drunken Brawl He Shot Me in the Back to coward to face me as I laid dying she came up to Me and Whispered In My Ear that She was Pregnant with My Child.My Last words were to Tell Him It is His So he want Hurt You. I made My Peace with God and I was Judged I was Born Inside the Womb of the Red head I was in Love with,Yes Now I became Her Red Headed Daughter and She Knew who I was in a Previous Life. I spent My Whole Life Taking care of the Woman who in One Life was My Lover and another Life was My Mother,Stranger Things have Happened I guess. The Sheriff was Shot a Short time Later By another drunk Who Out drew Him. Wait you say You Do Not believe in Re-incarnation. So What is this thing we call Resurrection? You were taught that you Only get one Chance at this game called Life then you die and you get to go to Heaven forever and ever or if you were a bad Boy or Girl then you will Burn in Hell forever and ever,This is what Most Christian Families were taught,Right? This is How a Few in Charge can control the mass of People, remember every person is either a leader or a Follower Which are you? Every Person is either a Predator or a Victim again Which are you? Its Your Choice when only a Few In charge can control a mass of People they have to use Fear.So Say for Example,Your grandma Dies,Is She In Heaven With Jesus right now or Is She Still In the Ground Waiting on this Future Rapture to Come? Is Adam and Eve Still In the Ground Waiting on this Future Rapture to Come? Is Noah and His Family all Still in the Ground waiting on this Future Rapture to Come? Millions,Billions and trillions of different People all with a Different Fingerprint all dying from this Physical Flesh and Blood Mortal body are they all In the Ground waiting on this Future Rapture to come? Or are they All Up in Heaven right Now all with their Own mansion? Can You Do All The Different Things you would like to do in only one lifetime? You Hear about this Past Life Regression and Hear about People remembering things they have done in a Previous life does that make sense? What did The Real Jesus Christ teach? He asked His Disciples "Who Do People say I am?" One of the Disciples Replied "Some say you are Elijah." How can Jesus Christ be Elijah? when He Has been Dead for a Hundred Years? Another scenero,Jesus was walking with His Disciples and they Came upon a man Born Blind,One of His Disciples asked Jesus "Who Sinned,This man or was it from His Parents?" Obviously The Man could not have sinned in this lifetime if he was Born Blind they believed that People have a Disease or a Problem because they were being Punished by God for something they have done.This is What they were taught,All They Know is what they were Taught. All They Can Teach You Is What they were Taught so Most of the People during this time period believed if you have a Disease or Blind,Cripped its because you are being Punished by this God. Jesus answered "Neither" Showing that In One Life you get to Experience one thing,In Another life you may get to Experience something else. I can Write a Book about what its like to Be Born Blind versus being able to see then going blind and all the Difference and you can read this book and get a lot of the Feelings but until you actually Walk the walk and talk the talk and actually Experience these things then a Book will Not answer all your questions. Jesus was telling them this man chose to Experience this,Maybe He has lived many lifetimes before and Now He wanted to Experience what it would be Like. Can You Experience all You would like to Experience in one Hundred lifetimes? No There are so many Job opportunity so Many different skin color,Different Languages,Different Cultures Rich,poor,different Diseases different Illness different everything. What are you going to do in Heaven forever and ever? Is Saint Peter going to Meet you at the Pearly gates? Will a Physical Gate keep a Spirit/Soul out? Can you Eat in Heaven? I would like a Big Chicken Fried Steak with Mashed potatoes and Gravy over everything and a Big Glass of Sweet tea with Lemon,Can I Have that in Heaven? Who is going to Cook it? Who is going to Kill The Cow? How do I pay for this in American Dollars? Pesos? What language will We all Speak? Do We Push one for English,Two for Spanish? What button do I Push for Russian? Japanese? French? Can I get Married? If the Islam and Others say I can Strap a Bomb to My self and Kill My Self and as many as Possible I will Get Twenty Wives so How many Wives do I get? In My Younger days a Friend showed me a Playboy Magazine with these Identical Twin Sisters Blonde hair,Blue eyes Perfect body,Perfect everything so Can I Have these Two Identical Twin Sisters? That would be My Heaven,Would it be There Heaven? What Would you do with 20 Virgins anyway? Sure it would be fun for a While but then,Guess What, They are no Longer Virgins so Now You Have 20 Wives all Jealous of Each other saying you Love Her More then You Love me and They All Get Pregnant so Now You Have Twenty Little Babies and One starts crying and He wakes the others Up so Now You have 20 Crying babies with dirty Diapers so Is God Going to Give you a Mansion? Why? What did you do to Deserve a Mansion? Do You Realize How Many Million, Billion, Trillion of People are out there just Now in this Lifetime so Imagine all the Previous past ten thousand years all the people born,died and is that it? Sure it makes sense to Control you by telling you if you are a Good little Boy then you will get a reward so they are saying all this to control you.The Few Smart Enough To control the Majority. Who Gets to Be In Charge? It Used to Be Only the Strong survive, now its a Democracy a few People saying the right thing at the Right time to convince you to let them rule over you.Why Do We Have Wars? We are Jealous of What they Have and Want it so we Just take it by Shear force or right now its all about the Oil. What used to be usless Desert land that no one wanted we are finding out that underneath that sand is a bunch of oil and who ever owns the land owns the oil so now our greed,which is one of the 7 sins is one reason why we are fighting. Another reason is we can not agree on whose Religion is right and whose Religion is wrong,Again its all about everything you Know is what you were Taught,They Can Only Teach You What they were Taught. Until we Understand that and tell our self. If We Keep on doing the same thing then we will Keep on Getting the same result,So If We want something else to happen then Maybe we Need to Do something different. Its the same with Religion,If We Keep On Believe-ing the Same thing then Nothing will Change. Eventually You Will Realize the Religion you were taught Maybe Part of it could be Wrong. What Part is Wrong? What part is Right? Who Gets to Decide? Does the Religion you were Taught Make Sense? Who Are You? Why Are You Here? Were are you Going? Can You Do All THe Things You Want to Do In One Lifetime? What Will You Do In Heaven Forever and Ever? You Have a Right to Ask Questions and Demand Answers Read My Books,Make Me Prove it to You,But realize You are Here for a Different Reason then I am Here You Have Million,billion,trillion of Different People all Here for a Different reason,All With a Different Fingerprint, all on a Different path.

What works for me will Not work for you What works for you will Not work for someone else.Can there be a Million,Billion,Trillion People all in Heaven right Now? Or Can there be a Million,Billion,Trillion People all dead with only one chance at life all waiting on this Future rapture and all being Judged at the same time.

Chapter Five:
Kosher
Food Law
Act Five
Scene Five:

The Old man is Talking:" There are People Out there who are Atheist,Who Do Not believe in a Creator God or Goddess and They Realize that Certain Foods are considered Clean and Certain Foods are Considered Unclean. Its not just a Scavenger food problem that only deals with a religion,The Jewish and Islam today still Keep these Levitical Laws,Why? Even Though Most People think we are Not Under the Law No More they do Realize that Certain Foods do have a bacteria so why are you eating it?" pause Back in the House, in the Kitchen Cooking as the Camera crew sets up we go into the dining room and set down for a casual meal. He says: "ok We will be talking about Kosher food or in the Holy Bible, the Levitical law. We all Know thru Common sense that there are certain Animals,Birds and Fish that are called Scavengers, Even some Atheist who do Not Believe in any God or Goddess understand that certain foods have a Bacteria that to eat it you have to cook it to a certain Temperature to kill this Bacteria, Does this Dead Bacteria just Disappear? does it just go away? no, It is still there,Hopefully it is dead but if you eat this scavenger food and this dead bacteria it is still going thru your stomach ,intestines,colon and thru your blood stream so now you understand why some People get some diseases. I want to share with you a True story that is very Important. A Woman ate some pork that was not cooked all the way thru,This Bacteria went thru her arteries and veins and some wound up in her Brain,the Bacteria started growing in Her brain and became a Tumor the size of a Big Golf ball,She went to the doctor because she was having fainting spells were she would black out,they did some test and scans and found the tumor in Her brain. They had to shave Her hair off,Cut a Big hole in Her skull.Remove the Tumor then she had to go thru Chemotheraphy because of the Chance of it being Cancerous. This woman had to go thru all of this ordeal all because she went to a Fast food Resturant and ate Pork. Why Do they call it a Fast food Resturant? Because they fix the food fast. The Holy Bible has Not Changed, God made it Very Clear their are certain foods that are considered clean and certain foods that are considered Unclean,Its not Rocket Science. I know You are saying well Paul said In His Version that now it is ok to eat what ever you want to. Are you a Follower of God or a Follower of Paul? Remember Paul wrote most of His Books around 60-70 ad about 30 Years after Jesus was Crucified. All Paul Knows is this Angel Blinded Him from His Bright Light and Told Him Now its ok,Sounds like the same Angel who Told Eve to go ahead and eat the Apple,Remember Lucifer is the Sun so If Someone Blinds you for three days could that be the Sun(Son) Lucifer or Satan or the Devil Remember you do have a Choice. Remember also the New Testament says over and Over "If you Love me then Keep My Commandments" So you say we are No Longer under the Law,We are saved By Grace,Then Why Is there a Judgment day If you are already Saved By Grace? What about the Ten Commandments,You Say We are No Longer under that old Law,What about the Commandment "Thou Shalt Not Kill" Are we under that Commandment? Of Course we can not go around killing people. What about the Commandment "Thou shalt not Steal" are we Under that Commandment? Of Course,You Can't go around stealing things. so Now we are under some of the Commandments but not Under others? Do You Get to Decide which Commandment you want to be Under and Which commandment your Not Under? Jesus said In Matthew Chapter five "I did Not come Here to Change the Law,Not one dotting of a i or a crossing of a t and anyone who does will Be least in My Kingdom". Wait you say what about the part in the Middle that was added? "I come to Fulfil the Law" What Jesus did was He Died on the Cross to Fulfil the Sacrificial Law. Before this anybody could do what ever they wanted to do if they had money. All they had to do was find a Innocent Animal and take it to the Rabbi,Why Should a Innocent Animal die for something you Done? Jesus did away with the Sacrificial Law. You are Not saved By Grace,But are accountable,Your Physical,Flesh and Blood Mortal Body Came from a Female and when You Die you will Go Back to a Female,We call Her Mother Earth. Your Spirit/Soul will Be Judged,"Every Knee Shall Bow and Every Tongue shall Confess." You Do Not Get to Stand before God and say well I was taught that as a Baptist once saved always saved and when I was 14 I was Baptized and they Told me I was Saved By Grace,It will Not work.You do Not get to Go to Heaven forever and ever according to what you did do then you go into a New Resurrected or Re-incarnated body and you get to Experience something else over and over Circles and Cycles.So Do You Keep the same fingerprint life after life after life? Millions and trillions of People born,live so many years then they die If every person ever born from the time of Adam then can you Imagine how many trillion of different fingerprints there are? Even if people use the same fingerprint in every life they are Resurrected or Re-incarnated in that is still a lot of different fingerprints look at the population of the World today for example and no two People today living have the same fingerprint and People have the Audacity to say there is No God or Goddess there is No Creator. Darwin says we came from a Monkey so does this Monkey Have a Fingerprint? We can Understand this Evolution Theory. We agree we are going thru this Evolution right now. Our Physical Mortal Flesh and blood Human body is change-ing all the time. Old skin cells die off and New Skin cells are born. We are not the same person We were a year ago. We have Pictures of Me when I was Younger I can see Evolution but I do not See Fish coming out of the water and sprouting arms and legs i do not See Monkeys change-ing to Human beings, sure some people do act like Monkeys and some even look like a ape or a Gorilla.For Evolution to work their way then we would have to see this change going around all the time. Yes,they are partly right. Our Creators made or

Created this Evolution to show they are change-ing. A Tree changes too what started as a Small acorn becomes a Mighty Oak tree but thru evolution the Mighty oak tree will Some day die and will return to our Mother Earth only to be born again and again. What gets me is Scientist that say Earth has been around Millions of years and Dinosaurs were Extinct thousands of Years ago was this from the Flood? Was there a World wide flood at one time or another? One of my Dreams I had was Kind of Like the Movie Back to the Future were a Silver Delorean takes off in the air and time travels into the Future or past. there were several H.G. wells Movies about time machines so its cool and maybe that was in My Subconscious but i was asleep.The alarm clock woke me up and I took a Shower,shaved ate breakfast,went to Work like I usually do.I pushed the garage door opener to see It was raining and Thundering and I was Driving My Old Red Volkswagen bug i had 30 Years ago. I backed out of the Driveway and started down the street,The Bug took off in the air and I time traveled in the Past. I wound up in Israel in the desert Right before jesus Was Crucified. I spent six Years there I could Not Figure How to get back i Married a Widow woman who already Had two Boys and we had another son and another daughter. I found out they were some Wise men Looking for this messiah so i went with them to see him.I was one of over a Thousand People who got to See Our jesus Christ,the Yahshua Crucified on the Cross,Everyone Believed in the Last Minute He would Call a Thousand Angels to Rescue Him and he Did have the Power. I could Not say anything so In My Silence I watched from a Distance. Could i have Lived during this Past Lifetime? Was My Fingerprint the same Fingerprint I have today? I went back Home after it was Over and went to Sleep. I woke Up the next Morning to the Sound of the Alarm clock waking me Up,Startled I jumped out of Bed Looked at my watch and the day and realized during this 8 Hours of Sleep I lived six Years of My Life, I could tell You In great Detail all the Little things I done each day,My Childrens name, the Sheep I was taking care of, My Wife of Six years going thru the Birth of each baby and Not Having a Hospital to take her to and seeing My baby Boy and Baby Girl being born and watching them crawl on the floor and learning how to walk. How Can I remember Six Years in one 8 hour Night? in this other World, Time does not mean anything, a day is as a Thousand years i remember reading that somewhere in the Bible so the Dinosurs could be Living for millions of years and that would be Just like a Month or Two,Did these Cave man have fingerprints also? Are we the Only Civilization that has a Fingerprint? When I woke Up and I realized it was Only Eight Hours gone by and I knew I had to go to work so I took my Shower,ate my breakfast and pushed open the garage door Opener to find it was Thundering and Raining. I hopped in My Red Bug and backed out of the Driveway and Paused. Do I want to Put this in Forward and Take a Chance on Going back in time? It was Pouring down rain I put it in Gear and drove back into the Garage and Closed the Garage door Opener I called in Sick and went back to bed. I had some sick time built up and I did not want to take a Chance going into the Past and Spending six Years,Yes It was Fun, Learning a New Language Trying to Learn a New Custom, marrying a Beautiful Woman and Having Two Beautiful Children, could that be Me from a Past Life? What Happened? Did i get Killed? How could I have Lived

Six years In One 8 Hour Period? I Thought about writing a Book about my Ordeal but Realized there are so many Other Books about people who have Time traveled in the Past or In the Future and their World was a Lot More Exciting so probably no one would read it they would Think I just Imagined it and had a Dream from My Subconscious Imagination. The sad Part was I felt Like I was There and I saw My Saviour Jesus Christ being nailed to a Cross and Feeling His Pain Knowing I can Not Say or Do anything to Change History. Why Me? Millions and Billions of people out there Thousands watching as Their Saviour Died on the Cross or so it seems i know the truth,The real Jesus Christ did Not die he Lived another 40 More years He traveled from Town to town teaching God's Laws of the 7th day Sabbath,the Kosher food laws,the re-incarnation Laws and the Goddesss the Shekhinah. The World did not want to Hear what he was saying two Thousand Years ago and the World does Not want to Hear the truth Today,Why? Because the God of this World is still Lucifer and Lucifer wants you to Worship on Sunday the 1st day of the week just to show that he is the Ruler and he wants you to go ahead and eat Scavenger foods this Helps Keep the Population down by creating bacteria and a early death. Can you Imagine if everyone in the World stopped eating scavenger foods then so many thousands,Millions of Peopkle would not be sick,Doctors would Be out of a Job and People would be actually Living longer Heaven Forbid that, You have to Control the Population one way or another thru some disease or start another Big war. "

Chapter six:
The Messiah Ha Mashiach
Act six scene six:

The Old Man is Talking:" If you have read this Much of this Book and Have read any other of My Books you will see i say the same thing over and over in various Books,Why? How do you Remember something? Only Thru Repetitions right? When You Study for a Test then You Go over the same thing again and again, Actually if you have read the first four Books of the New Testament then you will realize these are Four Different People, Matthew,Mark,Luke and John all Writing in a Lot of Chapters saying the same thing. Why Is this Important? Because the Early People wanted to make clear the Life of this man called the Son of God or the Son of Man. Who was the Original 13th Warrior? If Jesus had 12 Disciples trained to Help teach People good and Evil then Jesus(Yahshua) was the original 13th Warrior.Who Will Take His Place? Who will Go out there and Teach People the Difference Between good and Evil? I am but One Man,The Crazy Rebel Preacher Who Had Long hair and a Beard Like John the Baptist His Cousin but Now thru the Years Shaved it all off because i was Pulling My hair Out trying to Figure out How to Fight these demonic Forces." Pause Back in the Living room, new day, new scene, the camera crew are here setting things up. The Demon that went into my body that first day has been gone,the Tattoos are still here, a constant reminder of the Mark, maybe not of the beast but in reality who created the Devil? If God created everything then did God Create Lucifer? Why? How do You Know if something is good or Evil unless someone Teaches you? What better Teacher then Lucifer Him self,Remember you Do Have a Choice. They are ready, the Microphone is attached to my shirt on with the show: "This is Chapter five of the sixth in the series in this Documentary we titled Fingerprints. Everybody knows the Holy Bible is a Bunch of Individual People telling you Their Version of What they Think actually Did Happen,That is Why its called a Version. If You Accept the Version out there today then Jesus Christ Can Not be the Messiah.The Ha Mashiach.Everybody Knows the Messiah or the Ha Mashiach Has to come from the Tribe of Judah,the Lion of Judah. Why Would God Pick Joseph, Knowing He was from the Tribe of Judah,With the Right Bloodline and the Right Dna then Not Use Him? If You Accept the Version going around today then they are telling you that the Spirit of God By Passed Joseph and went straight into the Virgin Mary. Did God Marry the Virgin Mary? No She was already Promised to Joseph. What do You Call a Child born out of Wedlock? This is what the Jewish and Islam think of our Christian Jesus. According to our own Version then Jesus Christ can Not be the Messiah,actually if you accept that its this way then God would be Breaking His Own Laws of Deuteronomy 22. You Can Put ten People in a Room and Maybe you will get eleven different Versions who Is right? Who Is wrong? Who gets to Decide? What If the Churchs at this time wanted to Separate from the Jewish System? The New Jesus Christ would Change from the Old Laws Bringing in a New Religion.They would call this New Religion Christianity awa y from the Control of the jewish Rabbi and their Power. The Leaders of this knew in their Heart that they did Not want woman to be Equal.They Have seen thru the Years the Troubles and Conflict develop. They Wanted a Male Dominant Creator with a Male Son Showing the Male Dominence. they Had to Hide the Goddess so now they called Her the Holy Spirit,whenever the Bible mentions this Queen of Heaven or the Shekhinah,they would change it to say the Comforter or the Holy Ghost with a male Tone.Only a few remnants of the Old Goddess Remains a few scriptures withstood the Powers of the Devil who Tried to control this New Religion by First Killing this Messiah to forever shut Him up.Everyone Knows this World is Controlled By Lucifer,This is His Domain,When God Brought forth a New Son to Help Change the World and Show Us the Right Path to Follow did we Follow it? No Do Not Blame Jesus he was Only Here for a Short 33 years,Yes He Did Impact this Olde religion and He did Create this New Religion but Lucifer Is still Involved in making sure we are Still Scattered and Confused. What Really Did Happen was What Our Father God and Our Mother Goddess did do and Lucifer could Not stop them. The Only Two People in The Whole world Who Has More Power than Lucifer is His Creator,Our Father God,Yahweh and Our Mother Goddess,Shekhinah. God Did Pick Joseph so that Jesus would Be the Messiah,the ha Mashiach. The Spirit of God went into Joseph,not the Virgin Mary. The Holy Spirit Went Into The Virgin Mary, Then Joseph and the Virgin Mary Did what all Married People do and that is Have sex, God Told us to be fruitful and Multiply. A Child was born from that Perfect Love,Perfect Trust, the Son of a Carpenter,With the Right Bloodline and the Right Dna to Be the Lion of

Judah. the True Messiah,the Ha Mashiach. Thru the Years Lucifer tried to Change the Holy Bible By putting Different Versions and saying well Luke said this or John actually said this you can realize there was no TV no Radio,No Newspaper,No Fancy Hospitals things were Pretty rough back then most of the things were handed down from Father to son or Mother to Daughter. Lucifer is still In Control of all the Religions. He wants you to Worship Him on His Sunday Because He Is the Sun God,The true First Born Son of the God and Goddess Which is true,This is His World,Like it or Not,Believe it or Not,Does Not Matter. Jesus Understood this so he Had to Speak thru Parables,the Average person would not understand but those in tune to the Word of God and the Goddess would pick up on the true sayings But the average Person Today is Just as Gullible as the Average person two Thousand Years ago. People Only Know what they were taught. From the Day you were born if you were taught that there is Only a Male God and You Only get one Chance at this game called life and You Will die and get to Go to Heaven forever and ever and You are told this day after day Year after year then you Believe it and Its hard to Get People to Wake Up and accept the real Truth. The Big Question Is Its Not Wether We are Right or Wrong,Its Not wether your Version of the Holy Bible is right or Wrong.Its Once you realize We are right because It Really Makes sense then What are you going to do? You Have a Right to ask Questions You have a Right to Demand Answers Prove me Wrong. I been Fighting this for sixty Years. I was Just Like you I was Told this is the way Religion was,Its good enough for My Parents so its good enough for Me." We pause because its Lunch time,The Pretty Girl in the Boxing arena in the Bikini Shows the big sign One Hour Later."So Now We want to talk about Judus Iscariot everyone knows Him as the One Person who Betrayed our Jesus Christ but in Reality He Loved Jesus,He Knew He was the Son of God and He Knew one day that the World would Understand this. He was Tired of Running from one city to another. People were Jealous of Jesus,They Had a Big scam going and this scam was making them very Rich. Jesus was trying to Teach Mankind the truth and they Had to Kill Him to Silence Him.Judud Thought In His Mind that if They Tried to Kill Jesus then at the Last Moment he would Bring a Legion of Angels Down to Rescue Him. A Lot of People Thought the same thing,Jesus Did have the Power to Show the World this was what needs to Happen,But God also Realized Mankind was Killing Innocent Animals all in the Name of Trying to Get away with something. God had to Put a Stop to this Sacrificial law and the Only way this Society would allow this and this Lucifer allow this was for God to allow His Son to Take the Ultimate Sacrifice. Lucifer allowed Jesus To die thinking He Finally Silenced this Rivalry but God Allowed this Sacrifice to Show that we Can Not Do What we Want to and then Kill a Innocent Animal for something we Did, So Did it backfire for Lucifer? In a Way Lucifer Got What He wanted,He Is still In Charge,This is His Domain Like it or Not This is His World. Sometimes our Father God or our Goddess Mother steps In to show they are still around but You are Allowed to Do What you need to Experience During this Particular Lifetime. When You Look at the Big Picture and Finally Realize there are Million, Billion, Trillion different People all On their Own Path, all doing what they need to do to Experience what they need to do during this lifetime and each person having to do what they need to do to Experience all the Different things they want to do and then something Happens. Some Drunk runs a red Light and crashes in your car and accidently Kills you. Did you get to Experience all the Things you wanted to Do during this lifetrime? No, Why? Some Drunk ran a red Light and Killed Me. So Now Your Physical Flesh and blood Body is dead and your Spirit/Soul is Judged its Not Your Fault you still got a Lot of Things you wanted to do but Life is a Bitch then you die, so Now what Happens? Do You Have to Start all Over go into a Womb and Spend 9 Months Upside down surrounded by Water then come out Kicking and Screaming and learn How to Talk,walk and go thru learning the ABC of Life. Can you Just go to The School and say give me My High School Diploma? No You Have to Go thru your 12 years maybe you can Skip a Year or Better Off You Maybe allowed to Attach your self to another Flesh and Blood Human who is trying to do Similar things to What you were doing. This is what we call a Split Personality a Spirit/Soul attaches to another Spirit/Soul,Kind of like a jeckyl and hyde but sometimes one is Not Good and One is Not Evil so can we Have a Person with a Split Personality? Can We have a Person With Multiple Personality? Can these be Entities that did Not get the chance to Experience all the things they wanted to Experience and their particular life was Shortened due to a Freak Accident? Can there really be Freak Accidents? Is everything in Life Pre-ordained? Can that guy who was Drunk run the Red light Because that is what He Needed to Experience?maybe He Needed to Experience Going to Jail,Going to Court, being Sued and go thru the Humiliation of Knowing your Drunken attitude Killed a Family and Changed their Life and Now Its Change-ing your Life. How Many People are Now affected because of One simple Ordeal?One of My Other Books We used the Scenero of every Body in the World on this imaginary Spiral Staircase Millions,Billions and trillions of people all on this spiral staircase it does not matter who you are or how many Lifetimes you have lived You are some where on this Spiral Staircase. You Can Look up and see others that are Higher then you are you can be Jealous or angry but you realize maybe they are Higher than you because maybe they know things you do not know maybe you graduated from High school and maybe they have a bachelors degree and then you can look down and see others below you and you realize that you are Higher than they are maybe you Know things they do Not Know. The Crazy thing is you can come back in two Years and see Some Poeple are still At the same Place,They are Not Moving Up at all but on the Other hand they are not Moving down. At one Point in My Life I was way up on top soaring with the Eagles and I Had a Bad car Accident that Knocked me all the way to the Bottom,Yes I had to Get Knocked down to the Bottom,I needed to Lose Everything to wake me Up and realize What I did have. I hope No one has to go thru that but I realize that sometimes we need to Go thru these Obstacles and failures what was it that God said He Built You Mountains so You would Learn How to Climb?. I had to Get Everything Taken away from Me to realize What I did have Its a Long way from the Bottom back to were you were at. We are not satisfied to stay at one step on this spiral staircase. We can Look up and Imagine why God gave me two arms,One is to raise it Up and Hope someone on a Higher step will see my arm and teach me what We need to know to Move up that One step. My Other arm is reaching down to someone below me to Hopefully teach them how to Move up one step Higher. We are Not Looking up,Our Faith has my one arm holding up but We are looking down at my fellow Brother and sister Trying to teach them what they need so they can grab my out reached hand and pull them self Up. That is What this book is We are Reaching out to My Fellow Brothers and Sisters. You do Not see it But My Hand is Out there Ready for you to wake up and Realize some of the Things We are saying Maybe are true. Are you ready to Grab my Hand and Pull Your self up one step Higher? If So I am Looking at you and You will Have Only one hand sticking up but your other hand is reaching out to someone else below you to Help pull them up to at least were you were Thats whats its all about Its called the Brotherhood. Its good for our Brothers and our sisters both.End of Chapter

Chapter seven:
7th day Saturday Sabbath
Act Seven   Scene Seven

New Day New act new Scene New Clothes New glass of Dr.pepper Cold Drink in hand relaxing on my sofa." We waited till Chapter seven to talk about the Sabbath Because We Know that Our God Created this World in Six Days and He Rested on the 7th day. It was so Important to Him that He Put this in the Bible Not once but Twice and the One Commandment that Has More Words than all the rest Is Commandment Number four explaining that You shall Not Work,Your Wife and Children even your Slaves,Yes back then It was Customary to Have Slaves. They Had to have a Day of rest and God made it very clear that Saturday,the 7th day of the week was the day of rest,But then you have to realize the First born Son of God was Lucifer and he was the Sun God and He wanted Mankind and Society to Worship Him so in 313 ad He Made sure that the Roman Emperor Constantine did Change the Original 7th day Saturday Sabbath to a Sunday,the 1st day of the week Sabbath,Remember Its Still His World. This,I Believe started the Roman Catholic Church. So Now the Question is what happened during the 300 Previous Years from the Time Jeus was Crucified? Everyone Knows Its because of Jesus the Time was Changed from B.c.to A.d. and now we call it Before the Common era and after the Common Era because of so much difference in Religion. When I grew up the Baptist Called it B.c. which Meant Before Christ and A.D. after Death so What Happened during the 33 years he lived on this Earth? Did Jesus have a Fingerprint? Did He Only have one Chance at this game called life? Was He Really Killed that day? Some People say the Sponge they Put Up to His Lips had a Potion that Simulated death. We do Know the Roman Soldier was told To Make sure the People were dead because they knew the 7th day sabbath was about to Happen, They did follow that law if anyone moved after being stabbed then their legs were broken to hurry up the agonized death. The Roman Soldier stuck the Spear in the Side of our Saviour and the Potion knocked hm out to simulate death, They assumed He was already dead so they did not have to break His legs. After they brought the Body of Jesus down, it was a Matter of time before the Potion effects wore off but they also Knew If they walked around, People would recognize him and someone would go tell Pilate. They had to Disquise Him so they Cut off Most of His Hair,Shaved Him so He would look Different. I remember in My Younger days I was a Wild and Crazy Person I had long hair and a Beard plus all the Bad ass Tattoos to show my Rebellion. The Problem was Society Judges you by what you Look Like. It was hard for me to find a Decent Job,One day out of frustration I went into the Bathroom,Looked in the Mirror and I did Not Like what I seen,I shaved My beard off and cut some of my Hair,when I walked out of that Bathroom My Dog started barking at me,He Did Not Recognize me Even My Little Kids when I reached down to Pick them Up they looked at me and started crying i had to Hold them and assure them its still the same Me Inside it took a Little while to get used to the New me and even Doubting Thomas who Knew the Real Jesus Christ Did Not Recognize Him we all Know the Story so Jesus had to Flee the Town. Was Jesus actually Married? Yes Mary of Magdalene was His Wife. Did He actually Have Children? Yes Two Boys and One Girl did they all Have Fingerprints? Yes Are their Dna still out there? Yes The Children Grand children all the way down the Blood line of Jesus Christ is still out there. The Movie called the Da Vinci Code Talks a Lot of this Were did they get these Ideas from? They searched for the Truth,There are Spirit Entities out there today just like there was Spirit Entities back then.We all have our Guardian Angel watching over Us and sometimes we Want to Ignore what they are trying to Teach us so sometimes we Need to Go Back into the Womb,Learn a New Language, Learn a New Custom and Learn a New Culture so Can you Do all the Things you want to Experience in one Lifetime? You Have to Decide All You know is what you were Taught. Your Sunconscious will Only Accept What you tell it to Believe in, You Be the Judge At Least think about What We are saying I am either right or wrong. What part of what We are saying is Right? What Part of what We are saying is Wrong? Who gets to Decide if We are Right? Who gets to Decide If We are Wrong? I Have Nothing to Hide,If you are reading this then ask Questions send me a E-mail my e-mail address is melvinabercrombie@yahoo.com and My Church e-mail is brokenwingministry@verizon.net my snail mail address is Melvin Abercrombie 3230 Ridgeview rd Caddo Mills Texas 75135 if you are in the Dallas area Drop by actually I am about 40 Miles east of Dallas Texas I hope this will be the last book I wrote. I said that last time thinking We said all I needed to say then I have these crazy dreams and the spirit Tells me more stuff. In My Dream world if I am seeing,hearing and touching things then did I leave my Fingerprint there? I know I asked this before but I want you to think about this,Millions,Billions,trillions of different people thru out the World in this Lifetime so Imagine the last two three Thousand years how many different people all Here for a Different Reason going down a Different path why? Were are you Going? Were Have You Been? Have You Experience everything you want to? Did You Leave your fingerprint there? People Talk about the Tombstone they want on their Grave site they Put their Name,the Date they were Born and the date they Died sometimes the Only thing between these two dates is the Dash,People say

What is your dash? What did You Accomplish during this Lifetime? Did you Leave your Fingerprint? When you Stand before this Creator on your Judgement day How will He Recognize you from the Million, Billion, trillion others out there? He created this Fingerprint,He Knows the Hair on your Head. You See People in every Life going thru Disease, Sickness ,Cancer, Handicap,rich,poor,all walks of life all Cultures,all languages some because they did some bad things in their Previous life others because they Chose to Experience these things. what do you need to Experience? This Lifetime I learned a little about Patience and Perserverance i was always in a Hurry,Why? I wanted to Accomplish so Much in a Short time. Now I am More Relaxed,if I do Not get to see the seven Wonders in this Lifetime then I will Make it a Priority to add it to my Bucket List in My Next Lifetime. Instead of Doing what I want I Now ask God What does He Want me to Do. Sometimes the things I want and the Things God wants me to have are different so Now I learn to Accept what I have and Be Thankful and Let God Give me What He wants me To Have When He Feels I am Ready Remember there are Two Kinds of People in this World leaders and followers If you have read this book and want to be Involved in Helping build a Broken Wing Ministry in your area send me a E-mail I will do everything i can to Help you set it Up and Make it a legal Church Ministry Its up to you.Thank you for reading this Amen and Shalom

Chapter eight scene eight act eight: Duality 13th Warrior Today

Everyone is gone,the Camera Crew Is gone to edit the Film footage and make this into a Low Budget Documentary.The Old man Speaks: "No One wants to be the 13th Warrior,it seems we have decided the Number 13 as Bad Luck but Jesus Christ Had 12 Disciples and that made him the 13th Original Warrior. Maybe if He Had of Chosen twenty or a Different Number.We Do Have 12 Months in a Year and sometimes the Number 12 can be Good luck or bad Its How you were taught. Remember Everything you Know is What you were taught. Is there a Devil? Does He Rule this World? Is He a Male? We Created this Male Dominate Society wanting everything having Power to be a Male Species. We Over look that everything in Creation Did Come from a Female,Every Human, Animal,Bird and Fish Did Come from a Female,But our Male Chauvenistic Attitude that we are Man with Big Balls and Testosterone so we are the Rulers,Is it our Ego? Our Pride? Our Vanity? 2,000 Years later have we,as a Society and as Different Cultures Learned Anything? When We Look at 90% of the So Called Christians worshipping a Male God on Sunday,the 1st day of the week,Thinking we are saved By Grace and we Only get one chance at this Game we call Life and we get to Go to Heaven forever and ever and we can eat what ever Scavenger foods we want to then cry out because we have all these weird diseases and Cancers and we Die before Our time all because of our stupidity and Not reading a Simple book called the Holy BibleOr actually a lot of People will say they do read the Holy Bible but what you are getting out of Your Version is what you were Taught,Why Did Jesus Christ speak in Parables? He Knew a lot of People were Jealous of His Powers,Claiming to Be the Only Begotten son is What they say He did say But they are putting Words in His Mouth,Jesus Never Proclaimed to be the Only begotten son of a Male Dominant God. Jesus Knew the Devil was the First born son and the Ruler of this World,That is Why the Devil took Jesus On top of the Mountain to Tempt him and Test him finally What did the Devil say,Truly this is a Son of God,Jesus Did Pass all the test and even Lucifer admitted that Jesus was His Brother." I feel the Presence of the Ghost Camera,"She is still Here, constantly filming my every Move,Yes even when I go to the bathroom I feel her Presence. I realize She Is my Guardian Angel sent to constantly watch over me. she is Filming everything to document before our Creators everything. Remember When someone told you they felt their Whole Life Flash before you at that moment? This is actually What is Happening. I read this Book called Wisdoms and the First Wisdom Was called Duality,the Symbol for Duality is a Coin showing there are Two sides to everything,Good and Evil,Left and Right,Up and Down,forward and Reverse so If you Lok at your Life you can use that Wisdom to Make you a better Person You Now Realize you do have Good and Evil Inside of you Its a Percentage Just like If you Are a Male During this life then you would have the male Hormone Testosterone Inside of You but you would also have a Little of the female Hormone called Estrogen Inside You also. Scientist and Doctors have Proven this. I would Like to Think of when i was Young and the School Teacher was trying to teach us Fractions She would Draw this Big Circle on the Board and say this is a Big Pie so If You Cut this Big Pie In Half then you half this Line drawn thru the Middle showing Now you Have Two Halves of a Pie so two halves Equal a Whole. This is simple Teaching that a Child Had to Learn. I believe originally a Male God I call Yahweh and a Female Goddess I Call Shekhinah Created the First Children, we Call Arch Angels and They Both had Good and Evil Inside of them so When They Together Created Children then naturally the Children Had Both Good and Evil and they both had the Male Hormone Testosterone and Estrogen Inside of them. Now I want to Talk a Moment about these Hormones. A Long Time ago When I was In the Baptist,Christian Religion I was Taught that Being Gay or a Lesbian was a Sin a Abmomination against the Bible Teaching. Everyone has read the Bible story about Sodom and Gomorrah. I was Taught If you go to a Bathroom,Pull Your Clothes off and Look down and you see a Man then You Need to act like a Man,That is What you are during this Particular lifetime. Now we have the Hormones we can add if needed but hese is Only the Physical side of Us,Everyone Knows there are three sides to every Individual,Physical,Mental and Spiritual. I can see How Some People Maybe a Female in a Past Life and Having a Total Recall of that person and Carry-ing over some of these Emotions,Feelings and Baggage. i Know a Lot of gay People who Tell me they are a Woman Trapped in this Mans Body. Change-ing your Hormone By Adding the Steroid Testosterone will Help Physically but Mentally they still Believe they are still a Woman. We Know the Female Has the same Problem Thinking they are a male trapped in this Womans Body again now you are a Female in this Life,Get some Estrogen,Forget your past life,Enjoy Being a Female in this life and Experience what you need to Experience as a Female,maybe in Your Next

Life you get to ne a male or What ever you want but do Not Play God and Look down and not be Happy with what you are today. God Does Not Make Mistakes God made you a Female or a Male For a Reason You Need to Experience these and Not Create some diseases because mentally you Remember What you are in a Past life forget all the Past Life Drama,You are a Male Now act Like a Male,You are a Female Now,Act like a Female. Physically add Hormones,Mentally Seek Counseling Spiritually Be the Person God/Goddess created Enjoy each Life to the Fullest.Why are you a Male In One Life and a Female in another life anyway? Why Can't you just be the same Life after life? Then How do You Experience Different Things if you are a Cookie cutter life after Life would the World be Pretty Boring If You Knew Exactly What you are going to do in each Life after Life after Life? Being Gay or a Lesbian is not a New thing our Societies and Different Cultures have been Dealing with this Situation since the beginning. What is the Answer? According to God and Goddess we Were Created as Opposites a Male and a Female. The Only Way we Can Pro create is thru this One Male and One Female Marriage,Originally Sex was Created after a Couple gets married but today we think we are No more under these old laws and we have Lucifer to think for that.So If Lucifer was the First Born Son and he Is,He Is the Ruler of this World Like It or Not,Accept it or Not,It Does Not Matter he Is Here,This is His Domain God and Goddess Created Adam and Eve to give these Fallen Angels something to Rule over,They Stood Back and allowed The Fallen Angels something to do. Read Genesis Chapter Six,It says The Sons Of God Looked down and saw the Daughters of Man were Fair and they Took them Wives.and Their Were Giants in the Land. Were did these Giants Come from? We do Know there Were Giants Because we Know the Story about David and Goliath Right? Goliath was the Leader of all the Giants. That Means He had to be the Biggest baddest Meanest Giant of all of them,Right? Only the Biggest baddest Meanest Giant gets to be the Leader. Just like a Pack of Wolves they Have a Alpha Wolf or Alpha Dog which is the Biggest,Baddest Meanest Dog is the Alpha Dog and that is the Leader so Goliath was Obvious the Alpha Dog,Right? Sometimes in our Society,Our Culture we have a Alpha Dog as Our Leader He Needs to be the Biggest,Baddest,meanest Person around and He Gets to be the King,Right? You Have to Obey the King,He can't Be some Whiney Wimpy Kid Ruling a Great nation But that was what David was.He Picked up a Little rock and Hit Goliath in the Only Vulnerable spot right Between the Eyes. All Of His Armor did Him no Good,Everyone has their Achilles Heel their Vulnerable spot. What is your Weakness? Lucifer knows. He is the God of this World. He Is the First Born Son of this God and Goddess,Yes Jesus was a Important person.Just Like Hurcules was Born Half man Half God so to was Jesus Born Half Female and Half God to Do Away with this Sacrificial law and To Teach you the truth..Duality Teaches the Wisdom that Inside us If you take that Pie and Cut it in Half then Cut each Half into Half then you have one fourth times four so Inside of you Now You have this duality of Good as Being three Fourths and Evil as only One Fourth. If You are Created during this Lifetime as a male species then you have three Fourth Make Hormone called Testosterone and One fourth Hormone called Estrogen Inside of you. This is Normal. You Can Not go to a

Doctor or Surgeon and tell Him to use this Fancy Laser Surgery and remove this Evil Out of You or remove this Female Hormone Out of You.It can Not happen. We Have Figured this Hormone Thing out and Now we Can Take a Hormone Substitue and Change our Balance which is What some Weight Lifters and Body Builders do so they are Changeing their Hormone Balane with Steroids and we Do Not Know what the Long term affect will be. We also Found this Hormone called Human Growth Hormone and we Figured Out we can Put his into Our Cattle,Chickens and Other Food supply to Make them Stronger and Better and Now We are eating this and Changeing our Hormone Levels You can see 12 Year old Girls Developing breast and Young Boys being developed before their Time we Do Not Know the Long term affect on this will Be we are Playing God and Creating Sperm and Egg thru Artificial Insemination and we Will Eventually Think we are a God of some Kind. Lucifer and all His Cohorts are Just setting back Laughing their Butts off at the Silly Humans Trying to Be Gods. We Steal From the Mother Earth,Dig Holes in Her and steal Her Diamonds,Emerald,Gold,Silver,Oil and gas and Think It Belongs to You. We Do Not realize we came Into this world naked and with Nothing and we will Leave this World naked and with Nothing all the Material Things we Think we own will Not Buy us a Extra Moment Here on this Earth. Sure thru the ages some People Have Buried their Treasues with them in Hopes of Buying something in the Next Life can You Buy a Ticket to heaven? How Much Diamonds does the Ticket cost? How Many Oil Wells does a Ticket to heaven Cost? The Song says I got One Ticket to Paradise and He does Not Realize He does Not Need a ticket its There for the asking Jesus Tried to Teach us these simple truths,You Have Not Because you ask Not,Ask and You Shall Recieve But you have to Believe. If You Have the Faith of a Mustard seed You Can Move a Mountain. Do You Now Believe in a Male God Called Yahweh? Do You Now Believe in a Female Goddess Called the Shekhinah? Can There Be Equality? Can There Be Balance? Can there Be Harmony again? If You Accept the Fact that Lucifer Is the First Born son and the Ruler of this World,Even Though He was Cast out of Heaven and He is the Sun God this is still His World. Auriel Is the First Born Daughter She Is Mother Earth,This Is Her Domain. We see Tornados ,Earthquakes,Tsunami,Lightning,Rain,Thunderstorms,Hurricanes etc and we do Not realize that Our God gave the other Children Born Important Job Responsibilities and If You Ever get into Wicca the Worship of the Goddess You will See that the Four Directions are Ruled By the Arch Angels Like East is The Air and Ruled over by Raphael,South is Fire and Ruled over by Michael, West Is Ruled over by Gabriel and is Water and North is Mother Earth and Ruled Over By Auriel. When You Cast Your Circle of Protection You Are Calling on these Guardian Angels to Help Protect you. Broken aing Ministry Is the Only Church so for as I Know that Accepts Both the Male God yahweh and The Female Goddess Shekhinah as Equal. We accept the Teachings of Wicca combined with the Teachings of Christianity. We also Teach that Lucifer is the Sun God and Auriel is Mother Earth. They are the First Born Son and Daughter. You were Taught that the devil is Evil and You should Hate the Devil,Bind the Devil Curse Satan But In reality You are Only Making Him Stronger. God said To Love your

Enemies.Who Is Your Enemy? Is The Devil your Enemy? Then Love Him. How Do You Know if something Is Good or Evil Unless Someone Teaches You? What Better Teacher Than Lucifer Him self? Remember You have Inside of You Both Good and Evil Which one Is the Strongest? The One You Feed the Most. If you feed Evil,then You Become Evil,If you feed good then You Become good,Its Not Rocket Science its Normal Everyday Living life 101 Enjoy this Life Be somebody. Its Not Just Martin Luther King Who said it But You to Can Say it. I am Somebody,I may Not Be Rich But i am Somebody.I may be Black or White But I am Somebody. God and the Goddess Created You In their Image in the Image of Us You Have a Unique Fingerprint No one else has that so Yes You are somebody. Are you Ready to Become the 13th Warrior? Broken Wing Ministry needs Warriors all over the World,In every City every town to Help teach society the truths.Is this the Truth? What part of What I am saying is True? What part of What I am sayng Not True? All You Know is what you were taught,Your Subconscious will Only Accept what you tell it to believe in,They Can Only Teach you what they were Taught and Their Subconscious will Only Accept what they Tell it to Believe in Who Is Right? Who Is Wrong Who Gets to Decide?" My e-mail is melvinabercrombie@yahoo.com My Home address is Melvin Abercrombie 3230 Ridgeview rd Caddo Mills Texas 75135 if you Have read this and want to Help Build a Broken Wing Ministry in your area Let me know I can help you set It up. What would the World Be Like If we had a broken Wing Ministry In Every Town,Every City Every State and all Over The World? Would the World Be a better place if Millions of people Read My Books and Understood these Principles? Not because I wrote them,I am No Body,Just a Crazy Rebel Preacher Trying to Teach People His Version of the Truth. You Read the Book,You Decide Throw it in the trash can or Give it to someone else to Read.I see a Lot of My Books on Ebay and other places were People have Bought them,Maybe read them and are now trying to sell them thats cool You Pay six Dollars for this book and Maybe you can sell it and get some of Your Money Back. I Hope I told enough Cool Stories to get your Money Worth. So far No One has Asked for their Six Dollars back Thank you for reading this may our God Yahweh,and Our Goddess Shekhinah Bless you. May Lucifer teach you well,May Auriel our Mother Earth Show you all The Great Things in Our World and May our Jesus Christ(Yahshua) Show you the Law. Jesus Said "If You Love me then keep my Commandments" Shalom and Amen........